A Godly Shaking

A Godly Shaking

Don't Create Waves

Bill Vincent

A Godly Shaking
Copyright © 2014 by Bill Vincent. All rights reserved.

No part of this publication may be reproduced, stored in a retrieval system or transmitted in any way by any means, electronic, mechanical, photocopy, recording or otherwise without the prior permission of the author except as provided by USA copyright law.

Published By
Revival Waves of Glory Books & Publishing
PO Box 596
Litchfield, IL 62056

Revival Waves of Glory Books & Publishing is committed to excellence in the publishing industry.

Published in the United States of America

eBook: 978-1-312-59293-3
Paperback: 978-0692534793
Hardcover: 978-1-312-59291-9

REL012120 RELIGION / Christian Life / Spiritual Growth
REL108010 RELIGION / Christian Church / Growth
REL012070 RELIGION / Christian Life / Personal Growth

Table of Contents

Introduction

Lord, we thank you for all that you're going to do in the lives of all who read this. Let your power fall even as they read this. Lord, let your word pierce every heart, pierce every life, in Jesus' mighty name.

Jonah 1-9 King James Version (KJV)

Now the word of the Lord came unto Jonah the son of Amittai, saying,
Arise, go to Nineveh, that great city, and cry against it; for their wickedness is come up before me. But Jonah rose up to flee unto Tarshish from the presence of the
Lord, and went down to Joppa; and he found a ship going to Tarshish: so he paid the fare thereof, and went down into it, to go with them unto
Tarshish from the presence of the
Lord. But the LORD sent out a great wind into the sea, and there was a mighty tempest in the sea, so that the ship was like to be broken. Then the mariners were afraid, and cried every man unto his god, and cast forth the wares that were in the ship into the sea, to lighten it of them. But Jonah was gone down into the sides of the ship; and he lay, and was fast asleep. So the shipmaster came to him,

and said unto him, What meanest thou, O sleeper? arise, call upon thy God, if so be that God will think upon us, that we perish not. And they said every one to his fellow, Come, and let us cast lots, that we may know for whose cause this evil is upon us. So they cast lots, and the lot fell upon Jonah. Then said they unto him, Tell us, we pray thee, for whose cause this evil is upon us; What is thine occupation? and whence comest thou? what is thy country? and of what people art thou? And he said unto them, I am an Hebrew; and I fear the LORD, the God of heaven, which hath made the sea and the dry land.

Father, in your precious name let your glory fill everyone who reads this even now.
Touch every life. Touch every heart. Let your word bring life. Let it bring repentance. Let it bring deliverance. I speak the word of the Lord into every home right now. Spirit of God, let your fire fall. In Jesus' mighty name.

God is About to Rock Us

I want to release to you a message that I have given that I felt the Lord give me. I was praying about the this and the Lord spoke these words to me. You know when you study all the history there's been times and seasons where God has poured out His spirit in a phenomenal way. I don't know about you but I feel the stirrings of revival beginning to break out in our midst. I feel the fire of God beginning to fill pastors that are coming and testifying of what God is doing. People that are reading this are receiving miracles and deliverance. God is beginning to stir in our midst.

During great times of unrest and lawlessness. During times when men have looked and seen no hope, no future, God has looked upon the people who will touch literally the hem of His robe that they might be revived and He has moved in such power and glory.

I love the stories of Revival. Many saw such a move of God that men that were in the bars that used to be drinking their beer and when the glory of God rolled in these men that once drunk beer suddenly couldn't get the beer mug from off the bar side. Their arms were locked. These men that were mining men, men that cursed. You know the mules that used to carry the coal in the coal mines saw many of the men taught the mule to respond to curse words but when the glory of God rolled in these men that were getting saved no longer cursed and the mules didn't respond to them because they no longer would use curse words.

The glory of God so visited places that the police force suddenly had nothing to do because the crime rate dropped to nothing. So the police began to form choirs which are now known as the Welsh Choirs. Oh that God would visit Obama in such a way.

I look at the men of Charles Finney, John Wesley, Jonathan Edwards, John G. Lake, anointed by the Holy Ghost in fire. I think of Oral Roberts, A.A. Allen and Smith Wigglesworth. I think of the modern revivals of Argentina, Brownsville where God began to pour out His glory. In my heart I say, "God may we seize this moment. Come again, Holy

Ghost. Come again."

There were revivals where in a meeting and the glory of God fell. People began wailing out in repentance. People were laid, he said, like the slain. Like a battlefield as the spirit of God breathed in that revival. People attack revivals by saying, "what is all these people slain all over the place?" I want to tell you this is not a new thing. God's been doing this since Pentecost. This is not a new thing. This is a God thing.

Tired of Religion

You see there's a generation right now, I thank God for revivals of past, but there's a generation right now that know nothing of the move of God. The church, they have a conception, they have a perception of revival that God does it once every hundred years like it's some adrenaline shot in the arm. Revival is not an adrenaline shot. Revival comes when men and women that say, "Lord, we're tired of our ritual. We're tired of our religion. Come and touch us again."

God, we're going to lay down our formats. We're going to lay down everything we think we know and we're going to come before the throne of grace, humble ourselves, and say, "Lord, heal our land."

You see I want to tell you something tonight that might shock you. God doesn't hold back revival and then just say, "Well, there you go." God is ready to move every minute of every day of every hour of every week of every month. I tell you, we're not waiting for God.
He's waiting for you.

I've said this before but you don't make God nervous when you get hungry for Him. You don't make Him nervous when you say, "God, I want to see the cripple walk and the blind see.

God, I want to see the dead raised." And yet we get satisfied if we just have a good song on a Sunday morning. Woo, that was a good song. I want the glory. I want the cloud. I want the fire. I want the miracles. I want Jesus!

You see when you catch the fires of revival, when the fire of God truly gets on you, wherever you go revival comes. You see you can have an open heaven over a nation. You can have an open heaven over a family or a city but I want to tell you, you can have an open heaven over your life that wherever you go the fire of God goes. Wherever you walk miracles begin to happen.

When the fire of God fell on me it fell on me for a number of days. If you would've seen me you would've said, "That's a young man whose totally lost the plot. Always boisterous. He's too loud. Son, you don't have to shout." I remember when they used to say to me, this is a classic, "He'll be like me one day. I used to be like that when I got saved. He'll calm down. He'll mature." I used to look at those people and think, "I don't want to be like you. I don't want to be nothing like you." Sat there all depressed, bound in religion looking like an old prune. "Bless the Lord." I wanted the joy unspeakable and full of glory. Joy unspeakable.

River of God's Glory

I don't want stagnant water. I don't want some stagnant water when Jesus said that if you come to me out of your innermost being shall flow living rivers of water. I want to tell you we're living in a dry and thirsty land. I'm an
American right now. We're in a dry and thirsty land and I'm calling out, "Let the river flow, Holy Ghost."

Jesus said, "Whoever drinks of the water that I shall give him he shall never thirst but the water that I shall give him shall be in him a well of water springing up into everlasting life."
When people are near you, when they come in contact with you, they should feel life flowing out of your body. The River of God is beginning to flow right now.
Jesus said in Revelation 21, "I am the alpha and the omega. I am the beginning and the end. I will give unto him that is thirsty the fountain of living water of life freely." And yet, there are so many people that talk about revival, they talk about miracles, they talk about God. We want you to move but we want the power without ever the shaking or the rocking or the rolling. They say they want revival but they say, "Lord, don't make waves.

I'm fine as I am." There are pastors that are

reading this and you say, "Yeah, I want revival but Lord don't rock my boat. I've just got it how I want it. I've just got that big tither. He's tithing well, Lord. Don't make waves!"

Let the Waves be Released

You see just like Jonah the call of God is going out across America. Who will hear the call?
Who will hear the call? See my friend, without a move of God, without revival, America is falling down the path. Satan is stealing a generation. He's stealing your wealth. He's stealing everything you've got and I want to tell you God will not be silent but he will raise up a church that will stand against him with revival fire.

We don't want any waves. I remember when the fire of God fell in my dad's church. He went to Brownsville. He got hit with the fire of God.

See some of us are so dead in church we don't know the fire of God. We think something's going wrong when God is trying to make it right.

Some of you reading this are running away from the call of God. See the Bible says that Jonah heard the word of the Lord and he ran from the presence of God.
You see there's coming a time when there are people that God's been creating waves. You've run from the presence of God. You've

run from the presence of the Lord and you're wondering why everything's going wrong right now in your life. It's because you're exposed to what Satan has but there's a call. God is searching for you to say, "Come, I have a plan. I have a purpose."

A Deeper Calling

You see God had to find Jonah sleeping in the bottom of a boat and He had to rock that thing. You see God had revival on His mind. He had revival for a place that would totally turn it away from God. Ninevah was totally backslidden but God had restoration on His mind.

I want to tell you that God has revival on His mind for the United States of America. There are pastors that God is calling for you to lay down your ministry. To lay down all that you think you've got. See I want to say revival doesn't come without the shaking. God has to shake everything that can be shaken that that which remains is of the, that is of the Holy Ghost. You know Jesus gave me this scripture. He gave me Haggai 2:7 that says, "And I will shake all nations and they will come to the desire of all nations and I will fill this temple with glory says the Lord of hosts."

I want to tell you there's coming a shaking. There's coming a shaking of everything that can be shaken. There's coming a shaking to the church. There's coming a shaking to our economies. There's coming a shaking to our governments and to our leaders. Everything that can be shaken will be shaken.

You may be wondering why there's a shaking happening in your life. I want to tell you God's on your case. God's got His finger on you right now and some of you feel the enemy beginning to lash out at you. I want to tell you that is a sign that God's about to do a work in your life. You know God finds Jonah sleeping in a boat, running away from the presence.

Running away from the call. How many people are doing the same thing today. How many people are sleeping? I want to tell you some of you are going to sleep through revival. Some of you are going to sleep when God longs to do a work in your life. Some of you because you allow the whispers of Satan to tell you this is not of God you're going to sleep right through the moment of your visitation.

God is Turning Hearts

Sleepy, lethargic, critical. There are people reading this and you're going to make it your ministry to try and discredit moves of God.
There are people. You're already writing emails. You're already writing letters how much revival is not of God. But I want to ask you this question; where's the fire of God in your life?
Where's the fruit? Where are the miracles?
Where are the salvations? Don't destroy what God is doing. Get in, be shaken, that you might be revived.

I'm tired of people criticizing moves of God. Everything that God does is of the Devil. Well if it's of the Devil where's God? I want to tell you the Devil doesn't heal the sick. The Devil doesn't set the captive free. Satan does not heal the broken-hearted.

See I love the disciples when Jesus said,
"Let's get in the boat and go to the other side." You see the disciples didn't know it but there was a man so bound by Satan that Jesus had his eye on setting him free. The disciples get in the boat. Some of you started out and you were on fire for God, you got in the boat, and you were ready to go out into the deep. You

were going to have a healing ministry. You were going to win the lost. You were going to break the powers of hell. You got in the boat and suddenly the storm began to come and the boat began to rock.

You see revival means that sometimes God's going to rock you. Pastors you've got to let go and let God. You got to stop taking hold of what you think you know and you say, "Who are you man to tell me how to move in church?" I'm nobody. You know more than I'll ever know but I know this; that if you let the fire of God fall in your church He'll shake, He'll rock everything, but in the end it will be overflowing with the fruit of the kingdom of

God.
See the Bible says that Jesus said this, "A wicked and adulterous generation seeks after a sign and no sign shall be given it except the sign of the prophet Jonah. And he left them and departed." See God is raising up men that have been shaken. Men that have had their boats rocked but by the time God has finished making waves and they yielded their lives that God could anoint them with fire. See I believe that God is raising up young men, young women, older men, older women that just like Jonah will walk into a city and say, "repent."

We're going to see whole cities turn to God. We're going to see whole nations turn to Christ.

You know I love Paul when he writes, "It is doubtless. I count all things loss for the excellency of the knowledge of Christ Jesus my Lord for whom I have suffered the loss of all things and don't count them but done that I may gain Christ." The apostle Paul, everything that could be shaken, everything that could be rocked was rocked. But I love it when later he writes, "That I may know him. That I may know him and the power of his resurrection."

You see revival means when God so puts His fire on you some of you are so full of head knowledge but God wants to rock you and shake you and everything you think you know that He might put His fire on you. Just like the apostle said, "Silver and gold I have none but such as I give to you." In Jesus' name. In Jesus' name. In Jesus' name. In Jesus' name.

You can't give what you don't have. You can't tell God how He's going to touch you, when He's going to touch you. You just got to say, "God, make waves until I don't even look the same." That I may know him and the power of his resurrection. God Give me my mountain! Your mountain is your key to become who you are supposed to be.

See God is rocking the boat of the church right now. There are ministers that say God doesn't heal anymore. That it's all hype and it's all emotion. But God's going to rock, shake and break everything wide open. Just let Him do it.

About the Author

Bill Vincent is an Apostle and Author with Revival Waves of Glory Ministries in Litchfield, IL. Bill and his wife Tabitha work closely in every day ministry duties. Bill and Tabitha lead a team providing Apostolic over sight in all aspects of ministry, including service, personal ministry and Godly character.

Bill is a believer in Jesus Christ in the fullness of power with signs and wonders. Bill has an accurate prophetic gift, a powerful revelatory preaching anointing with miracles signs and wonders following.

Bill Vincent is no stranger to understanding the power of God, having spent over twenty years as a Minister with a strong prophetic anointing, which taught him the importance of deliverance by the power of God. Bill has more than thirty prophetic books available all over the world. Prior to starting his ministry, Revival Waves of Glory he spent the last few years as a
Pastor of a Church and a traveling prophetic ministry.

Bill Vincent helps the Body of Christ to get closer to God while overcoming the enemy. Bill offers a wide range of writings and teachings

from deliverance, to the presence of God and Apostolic cutting edge Church structure. Drawing on the power of the Holy Spirit through years of experience in Revival,
Spiritual Sensitivity and deliverance ministry, Bill now focuses mainly on pursuing the Presence of God and breaking the power of the devil off of people's lives.

His book Defeating the Demonic Realm was published in 2011 and has since helped many people to overcome the spirits and curses of satan. Since then Bill's books have flooded the market with his writings released just like he prophesies the Word of the Lord.

Bill Vincent is a unique man of God whom has discovered; powerful ways to pursue God's presence, releasing revelations of the demonic realm and prophetic anointing through everything he does. Bill is always moving forward at a rapid pace and there is sure to be much more released by him in upcoming years.

Other Books

By Bill Vincent

Overcoming Obstacles
Glory: Pursuing God's Presence
Defeating the Demonic Realm
Increasing Your Prophetic Gift
Increase Your Anointing
Keys to Receiving Your Miracle
The Supernatural Realm
Waves of Revival
Increase of Revelation and Restoration
The Resurrection Power of God
Discerning Your Call of God
Apostolic Breakthrough
Glory: Increasing God's Presence
Love is Waiting – Don't Let Love Pass You By
The Healing Power of God
Glory: Expanding God's Presence
Receiving Personal Prophecy
Signs and Wonders
Signs and Wonders Revelations
Children Stories
The Rapture
The Secret Place of God's Power
Building a Prototype Church
Breakthrough of Spiritual Strongholds
Glory: Revival Presence of God
Overcoming the Power of Lust
Glory: Kingdom Presence of God
Transitioning to the Prototype Church
The Stronghold of Jezebel
Healing After Divorce
A Closer Relationship With God
Cover Up and Save Yourself
Desperate for God's Presence
The War for Spiritual Battles

Spiritual Leadership
Global Warning
Millions of Churches
Destroying the Jezebel Spirit
Awakening of Miracles
Deception and Consequences Revealed
Are You a Follower of Christ
Don't Let the Enemy Steal from You!
A Godly Shaking
The Unsearchable Riches of Christ
Heaven's Court System
Satan's Open Doors
Armed for Battle
The Wrestler
Spiritual Warfare: Complete Collection
Growing In the Prophetic
The Prototype Church: Complete Edition
Faith
The Angry Fighter's Story
Understanding Heaven's Court System

Web Site:
www.revivalwavesofgloryministries.com

www.ingramcontent.com/pod-product-compliance
Lightning Source LLC
Chambersburg PA
CBHW052309300426
44110CB00035B/2321